DISCRIMINATION AND RETALIATION

AT THE A.R.C.

The true colors behind the red and white.

Author

Thomas J. Pledger

February 2, 2016

Thomas Pledger
Send all inquiries to the following e-mail.

Pledger.thomas@yahoo.com

Thomas Pledger

City of Publication:
Rome, Georgia

First edition: February 2016
The characters and events portrayed in this book are true and based on facts.

ISBN-13:
978-1523874651

ISBN-10:
1523874651

Dedication:

For my father whom taught me to never back down.

Rev.

Howard S. Pledger Sr.

Discrimination can happen to anyone and all races. It is no longer a black or white issue. We as a society are always looking to the past for a definition of what discrimination is. In today's society, you cannot always judge a person by their looks. For actions have always spoken louder than words.

CHAPTER LIST

Acknowledgements.

Thank you to my good friends C.H. and H.H. for all your help with this endeavor.

C.H. Artist and Cover Design

H.H. Editor

To all the people who said my case read like a book, this is for you.

Prologue

It is not rare to find this but I find it in my heart today to speak on this. Discrimination is no longer a white on black issue. In this book, you will read a story about discrimination from every race and against every race, even your own race.

Caucasians discriminating against African Americans.

Caucasians discriminating against Caucasians.

African Americans discriminating against Caucasians.

African Americans discriminating against African Americans.

Every one of these discriminations happened at the American Red Cross. In this tell all book, I will tell about the discriminations but I will not state the race of any parties involved.

What I will state is this, I am Caucasian.

It is with great pleasure, I present my new book.

DISCRIMINATION AND RETALIATION

AT THE A.R.C.

The true colors behind the red and white.

Chapter 1,

Getting Hired

Four years ago, I was hired by the American Red Cross. I was in need of a job and had no other offers. The date was September 8, 2011. I received and communicated with my then Supervisor through e-mails. She sent me these schedules for orientation.

THIS IS AN ACTUAL E-MAIL FROM ARC. I DID EDIT IT TO NOT NAME SOME PEOPLE WHOM ARE INNOCENT.

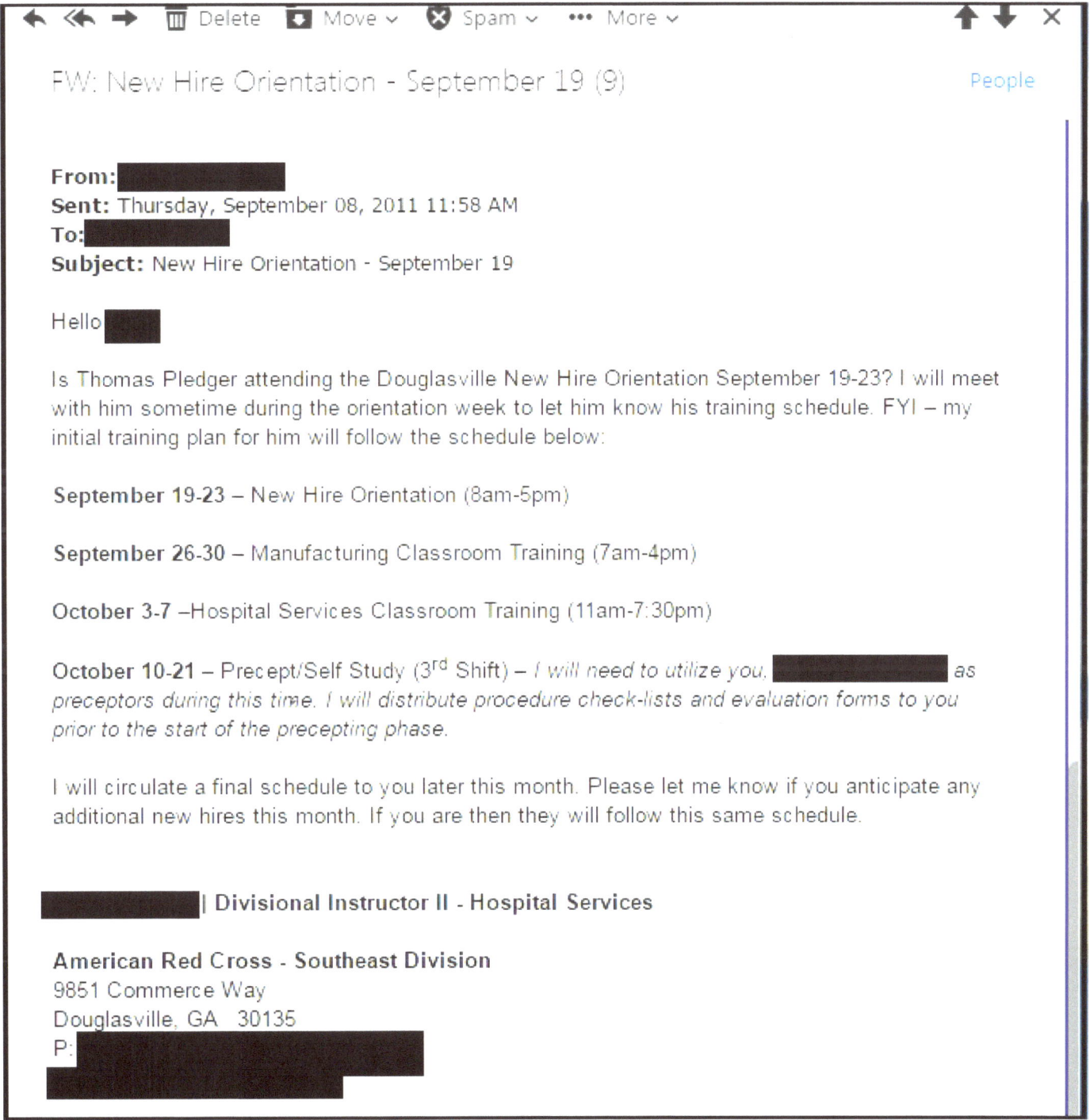

I followed the training schedule as it stated and was hired full time as a third shift Distribution Tech II. To put it simply, I put blood in boxes.

I remember the first thing my supervisor told me, "Document everything and always keep copies. This is for your own protection."

Taking her advice, I made sure that I made hard copies of any e-mails and always forwarded them to my personal e-mail account, in case I ever needed them. She told me to always make myself clear and never admit to anything without talking to my supervisor or my lead tech.

Chapter 2,

The First 8 Months on the Job

After completing my training, I walked onto the floor, where my department was, at American Red Cross. As I entered the door, I hear yelling at the back window. The supervisor from second shift was within a foot of someone sitting in a chair yelling, at the top of her lungs, at this young woman. Stunned and at a loss for words, I contemplated walking back out the door and going home.

I had to ask myself, "Is this the standard for how the American Red Cross is run?" I had been an assistant manager on a previous job and I knew I would never treat any employee that way.

These yelling sessions continued for the next 6 months on an off and on basis. After six months, the supervisor targeted and fired the young woman blaming her for the supervisor's responsibilities.

Here are the string of e-mails I sent to the Manager of Hospital Services and the Director at the time.

This is the first time I had ever seen or witnessed targeting for myself. It was and still is a mind blowing experience.

This e-mail was to the Manager of Hospital Services at the time.

From: Pledger, Thomas J.
Sent: Tuesday, March 13, 2012 3:17 AM
To: ███████████████████
Subject: ███████████

Dear █████,

I have very rarely spoken to you and I have not been able to touch base with you. I do want to tell you a little bit about ████████ from second shift. I feel that Redcross Second Shift will feel severe pains from her release from Redcross. █████████ was one and still is one of the hardest workers I have ever met.

I have heard a few things about why it happened but if any of it is true, I can tell you that Redcross made a mistake by firing her. I rarely think so highly of people that I would try to step in and tell truth where very little of it is spoken. What I can tell you is this.

█████████ was always the last person to leave from Second shift. When others would leave the floor, refusing to put up blood or stay past their scheduled times, █████████ was here working until all of the Second shift work was done. She made sure the trucks went out with every order and she made sure that the work █████████ should have been doing or helping her with was done.

I very rarely have seen or saw █████ deal with drivers or anything other than dealing with the office. Why is it that █████ was not helping? Being that it was not my shift, I felt it was none of my business.

But I will tell you this, █████ has been verbally abusing her crew and there is a witness to it. On a shift approximately a week ago, █████ was yelling at █████████, █████████████ witnessed this and asked █████ "Why is she yelling at you?" Several people in the building know █████ does this and noone is trying to do anything.

I have not been here but 6 months, I do feel that I will not be able to sleep tonight if I do not bring this to your attention on these 2 things. I feel that you should rethink the situation with █████████ and do a deeper investigation. I also think that maybe you should talk to some people on second shift about █████.

I am very glad █████ is my supervisor and works beside her crew the way she does.

I am not trying to tell you how to do your job but I am telling you what I know to be true.

Thank You for your time,

Thomas Pledger

↩ Reply   ↩ Reply to All   → Forward   ••• More

This is the e-mail I sent to the Director of A.R.C. in Douglasville.

Thomas Pledger

From: Pledger, Thomas J.
Sent: Wednesday, March 14, 2012 4:03 AM
To: ██████████████████
Subject: FW: ██████████

Dear ██████████████

I have only met or seen you a couple of times but I am forwarding this e-mail to you as I am trying very hard to follow chain of command protocols and the open door policy at the Redcross. I feel strongly about every bit of this e-mail and I wish to inform you of the things mentioned in this e-mail to ██████████████

I am asking that you try to do an investigation of second shift and ask a few people about what is going on with ██████████████ I have heard from several people that they are afraid of direct retaliation or being fired from Redcross for coming to Management about how ██████████████ treats them and others on Second shift. The employees on second shift in Hospital Services fear losing their jobs for making complaints about her.

In my first week here, working the floor in hospital services, I witnessed her harrassing an employee about a box that was put on the wrong route. This employee was severely punished for sticking up for himself. The employee told her several times it was not his hand writing but over and over again, she demanded he show her himself it was not true.

I am just saying Mr. ██████████, please investigate ██████████████ and the firing of ██████████████ is abusing authority and verbally abusing her employees.

Ask the employees about this and I am sure some of them will come forward for it.

Thank You,

Thomas Pledger

From: Pledger, Thomas J.
Sent: Tuesday, March 13, 2012 3:17 AM
To: ██████████████████
Subject: ██████████

Dear ██████████

I have very rarely spoken to you and I have not been able to touch base with you. I do want to tell you a little bit about ██████████ rom second shift. I feel that Redcross Second Shift will feel severe pains from her release from Redcross. ██████████ was one and still is one of the hardest workers I have ever met.

This is the e-mail reply I received from the Director of A.R.C. in Douglasville.

Thomas Pledger

From: ████████████████████████████ @redcross.org]
Sent: Wednesday, March 14, 2012 12:27 PM
To: Pledger, Thomas J.
Subject: RE: ██████████

Thomas,
First, my name is ████ to you (not Mr. ██████████) and I can't tell you how much I appreciate you stepping up and saying something to ██████ and me and letting us know your thoughts on this. I am sure you can appreciate the importance of the confidentiality we extend to everyone for their personal situations so while I cannot go into depth details of ████████ situation I can assure you I was personally involved in her situation along with ██████ and ████████ to assist her in being successful in her position. This is the same confidentiality I am extending to you now.

There is no one more disappointed at this outcome than me, I can assure you and the reason is because I saw ████████ exactly how you have mentioned above however there were several severe violations of policy that I just couldn't ignore. Part of my job is to ensure a coherent workplace that is fair to everyone and free from abusive acts both up and down the chain of command and I will do my job. There are right ways to deal with situations (like the path you have taken), there are wrong ways (which we will try to correct) and there are unacceptable ways (and failure to correct wrong ways is unacceptable).

So while you cannot see all the details of the situation we had to deal with I can only ask you to trust my judgment and also understand that all actions are run through the Human Resource department. We also attempt to do all we can to assist everyone to be successful in their individual duties but ultimately it falls to each us to correct our own performance. Additionally, other individuals in the department have not always done the "right" things but everyone gets feedback equally and is given a chance to correct any issues they may have.

So while I cannot give you details of other staff members issues, what I can ask you is to see if the department as a whole improves and to do your part to assist in that effort. You feeling strongly enough to send this email in the first place tells me that you care enough to help already. I truly appreciate it!

Thanks again,

████████

████████████████████ **Director, Manufacturing**
American Red Cross

Manufacturing Zone 7
Douglasville, GA 30135

In other words, A.R.C. covered up this targeting incident and I was told to shut up. They blamed the entire thing on the woman whom was fired.

In my own opinion, from what I saw and recognized, the supervisor over second shift targeted this woman. She verbally and mentally abused her. Then consistently wrote the woman up for violations that would later be used to terminate her. The manager, the director, and the supervisor all got away with it and then covered it up.

While I was there, the supervisor had the highest turnover rate of any supervisor in the building. If she did not like you or you crossed her, she would target you, build up as many write-ups as possible, and fire you. Each time the incidences occurred, Human Resources, the Director and the Manager of the department would back her. These behaviors continued for four years until 2015, when she voluntarily left the company.

A great many complaints were made about her targeting and nothing was ever done. This happened in every department and by nearly every superior from lead techs, to supervisors, to the manager, to the director and all of them would cover it up.

I had to ask myself again, "Is this truly the type of company I want to be associated with?" A question I would later regret not asking sooner.

Chapter 3

I Became Targeted

After I sent that e-mail, I began to be written up on a regular basis. Every time I turned around, it was something new. The lead tech over my shift would get me written up for the exact same things that she would allow other employees to do. I tried to tell my supervisor and every time, the supervisor would take the lead techs side.

As I became numb to the growing discontent, I decided to back down and let them have their way. This continued for three years. I finally gave in to the fact that I had to bring attention to what was going on. How could I do it?

The following response demonstrated how I would simply make a statement on each write up about targeting.

What I wrote in my comments was this, "The rules that apply to some do not apply to all."

Employee Verbal Warning

Employee: Thomas Pledger   Date of Occurrence: 081814

Job Title: Manufacturing Tech II   Department: Hospital Services

Describe the Event, Incident, or Deficiency: On 081814, 1830 Thomas was on task to ship FRAC for the day. The shift lead reported that as of 2330 Thomas had not started the task he was scheduled to perform. He had spent 4 hours making boxes, which significantly impacted the need to have these units processed before Mid-night to allow for other required duties to be performed. Due to the delay in performing his duties as required others had to increase their work load to compensate for Thomas not contributing to meet standing order requests, route demands, and productivity.

Describe Corrective Action to be taken by the Employer and Employee:

Thomas has been reminded that he is required to follow all assigned duties as outlined to include assisting in other duties as instructed and in a timely manner. To follow guidance as given by his supervisor and lead without delay. Thomas was informed to use company time wisely. If assigned duties are completed before end of shift, he has been reminded that he must utilize the rest of the time as a floater. The supervisor and lead will continue to monitor Thomas's progress and that he is complying with these instructions.

If Corrective action not met describe what further disciplinary action will be taken:

Failure to adhere to the guidance provided in this Verbal warning will result in an Employee Written Warning up to and including termination.

Employee Comments: _____

THE RULES THAT APPLY TO SOME DO NOT APPLY TO ALL!

I HAVE READ AND UNDERSTAND THIS WARNING NOTICE.

Employee' Signature: _____   Date: _____

Employee' Signature (Print): _____   Date: _____

Supervisor's Signature: ██████████████   Date: 08/19/14

Supervisor's Signature (Print): ██████████   Date: 08/19/14

This is what gets me, I was written up for insubordination for making boxes that we actually use to ship frozen plasma known as FRAC. How is this insubordination when I was doing my job?

Other employees could do as they pleased. They would spend all night doing less than 30 boxes of fractionated plasma. Yet, on the one night when I had to wait until midnight to start, I decided to make boxes until then. It became a problem with the lead tech. Putting it simply, she would go run and tell on me and not tell on other people.

I never knew if it was because I was white or if she just did not like me. This stuff happened for three years, until February 2015.

In February of 2015, I was called into the office for using the computer in the back of the work area. The lead tech had again targeted me on this matter. I was irate and refused to sign the write up. I went to my desk and sent an e-mail to my boss.

It simply read, "Did the lead tech tell you that another employee was on the computer, also?"

My supervisor whom was new at the time looked at the lead tech and asked her about it. The lead tech replied, "Yes, she was on the computer, too."

But she did not tell the supervisor about that person, only about me. I have to admit that this time, the supervisor sided with me. In less than one month, that lead tech left the shift. I believe that she left because she got caught even though she claims it had nothing to do with that.

Chapter 4

The Union and Debbie Drozda

By August of 2014, the people of the Red Cross had been fed up for some time with the policy changes, the targeting, the retaliation, and the firings. At this time some employees approached the Union. In the weeks that followed, over 80 employees had signed union vote sheets, as I like to call them. These are cards that you sign saying you want to vote on whether you would like the union to be voted in.

With more than an 80 percent margin asking to vote for the union, the American Red Cross, in Douglasville, Georgia, began their campaign to block the vote or turn people against the union, so they would vote no.

We had to go to meetings weekly about how the union was bad for the company. We were told that our insurance would change and that people would hate the union. It was then that people started doubting the union and whether we should vote it in. I listened to people talk and realized it was a 50/50 shot.

I wanted more information, so I sent out this e-mail to Debbie Drozda.

From: Pledger, Thomas J.
Sent: Tuesday, August 26, 2014 4:50 AM
To: Drozda, Debbie
Cc: Pledger, Thomas J.
Subject: Union

Good Morning Debbie,

My name is Thomas Pledger. I am a Tech II in Hospital Services at the Douglasville Region. With that being said, I must follow up with the information I was provided by you for the Union agenda and what it means to the Southern Region staff. By talking to you and sending this e-mail, I know that I am risking my job. But I feel that maybe if you just hear my situation, you could see that it is not about promises that are being made to us but about losses that the lower employees incur and how it means to take from us regularly. We feel it is not giving back.

The truth being told, yes, I was approached by a friend about this and yes I do feel it is a good move for the Southern Region to do this.

I did my own research on this subject before I made any decision and still have not completely made my mind up.

First, I compared rumors to fact. Rumor, Union employees make more money than those without an Union. I checked online and I can verify this with a story of my own. My brother in law works for a steel mill and has worked there around 15 years. He makes about 10$ an hour. He has no Union. My best friend works for a Steel Mill also in the same town. He has worked there for 13 years. He makes 17$ an hour. He has a Union. That is a true story.

Attached is the raise I got in 2013-2014. I got a 15 cent raise. Yes, I had issues with working and was on FMLA for a time due to my health. But really 15 cents, that might buy me a meal at Burger King each week. I average 130$ every 2 weeks in gas just to come to work. I drive 77.6 miles one way to get here. My car gets 36 miles to the gallon on gas. An average time of 1 hour and 45 minutes per drive. So for 3 hours and 30 minutes a day, I am behind the wheel of my car coming to work and going home. By the time I am done paying my bills, I barely have enough money to buy a few groceries to live off of for 2 weeks. I have little or no money left to even spend on my daughter. My average 80 hour work check, after taxes, child support, and insurance is $620-$640. I have no car payment and I am barely surviving.

When ARC cut the UL time out, that was expected. But to short wave our PTO and not give us a direct outlet for how much we accrue is wrong. Yes, you gave us a maximum amount but I have yet to find out if I will get less or more time per pay period in PTO. Truth be told, I am about 90% sure it will be less and at bare minimum, I will lose ½ hour a pay period. I feel that with a Union, I would have more information on this.

My health benefits, when you added a deductible to the health benefits at Kaiser, you should have just told me that health insurance for me would come fully out of pocket. I can NOT afford any deductible. As for what I said before, after I pay my bills, I am lucky if I have any money left to buy groceries... How can I afford a deductible on insurance if I can not eat? One has to come before the other. Yes, I do know that this is a basic move all companies are doing insurance wise, but that does not make it easier on me.

As for the reason that people here are thinking about going Union, look at all the memo's on the new changes. **The changes affect all employees except for Union and Puerto Rico employees.** People are talking about Union because, we had no say in the changes but the people in a Union are unaffected.

You can send me all the information you want on why this is a bad move for ARC Douglasville region, but for now, I choose to believe in what I know. First, I am not one of the few in ARC who make $80,000+ a year and can afford health care and the insurance changes.

I do not like change, I never have. I don't want another person telling me my job but I feel with a Union, someone may speak up for me. Who do I have to speak up for me now?

Thanks,

Thomas Pledger

The following is her reply:

From:	Drozda, Debbie
Sent:	Tuesday, August 26, 2014 2:02 PM
To:	Pledger, Thomas J.
Subject:	RE: Union

Tom,

Thanks for the email and taking the time to reach out to me to share your thoughts. I appreciate that you are doing your homework and keeping an open mind before making any final decision. I hope that all Douglasville employees will similarly keep an open mind and hear what we have to say about this union issue. In the end, I believe that when employees are informed about the facts of unions, most times they will elect to remain union-free and work directly with their management team, and I hope that will be the case here.

You have raised a number of thoughtful questions and points below, as have others. Because I want all Douglasville employees to share in the information, we are going to compile questions and points on a weekly basis and circulate our thoughts and responses in a "Q & A" format so that all can make an informed decision. We will begin this process this Friday, which will include responses to questions and points of yours raised below. Thanks, and I appreciate your feeling comfortable enough in sharing your email with me.

Sincerely,

Debbie

Debbie Drozda
Chief Manufacturing Executive, Zone 4
American Red Cross
180 Rustcraft Road, Suite 115
Dedham, MA 02026
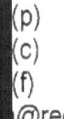　(p)
　(c)
　(f)
　@redcross.org

 American
Red Cross

From her reply, you can tell she did not care about me at all. First of all, my name is Thomas, not Tom. Second of all, all she did was confirm my true feelings, American Red Cross did not in any way care about its employees. The bottom line is all they care about. The people at the bottom can be walked on.

Question: Why does a non-profit company care about the bottom line?

Answer: People in charge will not get their salaries, hundreds of thousands of dollars, unless they prove they do not care about the employees.

Needless to say, I floated this entire e-mail to the union board members whom immediately saw that everyone they could talk to would read it. I did this, because I wanted the union to be a voice for all employees at the American Red Cross in Douglasville, Georgia.

By the end of the vote, the union was voted in by a margin of more than 70 percent of the votes. I generally like to think that was, because of my risk in floating this e-mail, but truth be told, I think everyone at the American Red Cross had grown tired of the policy changes, targeting, discrimination, and retaliation that goes on there.

I knew, as well as many, that from this day forward, after the vote, a target would be placed on my back. My time was limited and I would not be there long.

Chapter 5

Promotions Determined by Discrimination by Tracey Denson

I can remember three times I applied for promotions and was written up within two weeks of applying for those positions. The following is a particular write up that happened just after I applied for a Lead Tech job.

A lead tech position was posted, in February, when it was known the lead tech on my shift was leaving. I had been a good employee for the past eight months and that is significant.

American Red Cross policies state: that if you get a written warning within six months of applying for a promotion, that promotion will be denied. From these e-mails and this write up, you will see, I was treated massively unfair. I was written up, so that I would be denied the promotion I applied for without being interviewed.

This is the e-mail I received when I applied for the lead tech job.

Pledger, Thomas J.

From:	careers@redcross.etracksystem.net
Sent:	Monday, February 09, 2015 6:40 PM
To:	Pledger, Thomas J.
Subject:	Thank you for your interest BIO52322 – Lead Tech, Manufacturing

Thank you for your inquiry regarding our current job opening BIO52322 – Lead Tech, Manufacturing.

Your resume will be carefully reviewed against the requirements of our current open positions. Should your experience and skills match an available position, you will be contacted to arrange an interview.

EID:23

This is the e-mail I received when I was being considered for the lead tech job. As you can see, this e-mail is exactly 1 month after the first one. That is significant because it shows that they waited for a reason.

From: ▮▮▮▮▮▮@redcross.org [mailto:▮▮▮▮▮▮@redcross.org]
Sent: Monday, March 09, 2015 5:24 PM
To: Pledger, Thomas J.
Subject: Thank you for your interest in American Red Cross position of Lead Tech, Manufacturing, requisition # BIO52322

Dear Thomas Pledger,

You are being considered for the position of Lead Tech, Manufacturing. We will continue to update you regarding the status of your application.

Requisition #: BIO52322
Job Title: Lead Tech, Manufacturing

EID:37

Within that month, another employee was talked into applying for the job. He had been there a while and even longer than myself. The catch was, he had been given a written warning within 6 months of when the job was posted. However, by waiting until March 9, 2015, to reply to the employees whom applied, this allowed time for his written warning to fall off.

Then this happened eight days after I applied for this job. Tracey Denson ordered my supervisor to write me up.

This is the write up that I was given.

Employee Written Warning

Employee Name: _Thomas Pledger_ Date of Occurrence: _020315_

Job Title: _Manufacturing Tech II_ Department: _Hospital Services_

Describe the Event, Incident, or Deficiency: _____
Staff member failed to comply with ARC work rules regarding insubordination. On 020315, staff member
was instructed by 2 leads in the department and instructed by the manager to wait until the arrival of the
supervisor to address an issue. Staff member made the decision to ignore instructions given from all
authority. Upon arrival to the department staff member was instructed to ship FRAC. During the process of
shipping his complaint was that the units to be shipped were mixed PCodes that should not be mixed. Staff
member brought it to the attention of two leads who insisted that he wait until the supervisor's arrival to
address the issue. Staff member stated he did not feel as if the leads were correct in their suggestions and
or decisions & decided to contact the manager of the department. The manager instructed the staff member
to wait & follow up with the supervisor upon her arrival. Staff member decided that he would ignore all
instructions and seek guidance from another supervisor and manager in another department. When asked
why the disregard for all instructions given by the leads & manager of the department he had no reason.

Describe Corrective Action to be taken by the Employer and Employee: _____
Staff member has been reminded that he is required by ARC policy to follow instructions given by leads,
managers & supervisors. It was reiterated to staff member to follow guidance given without delay.

List Previous Warnings or Probation Notices (Date, Type, Outcome): _____
On 081814, staff member received an Employee Verbal Warning for insubordination. The next incident will
result in a final written warning including but not limited to suspension or termination.

Employee Comments: _____

I HAVE READ AND UNDERSTAND THIS WARNING NOTICE.

Employee's Signature: _Refused to Sign_ Date: _____

Employee's Signature (Print): _____ Date: _____

Supervisor's Signature: ███████████ Date: _02/7/15_

Supervisor's Signature (Print): ███████████ Date: _02/17/15_

Copies to Employee, Human Resources/Personnel File, Supervisor

As you can see, in this write up, the date of occurrence is 02/03/2015. Yet, the date I was written up is 02/17/2015. This is eight days after I applied for the lead tech job on 02/09/2015. Am I the only one that finds that a hard pill to swallow? I applied for a lead tech position and was written up for something 2 weeks prior...

The following is the e-mail I got on March 12, 2015.

Pledger, Thomas J.

From: ████████████
Sent: Thursday, March 12, 2015 4:57 PM
To: Pledger, Thomas J.
Subject: RE: Thank you for your interest in American Red Cross position of Lead Tech, Manufacturing, requisition # BIO52322

Hi Thomas,

Thank you for responding. However, I learned from HR that you are not eligible to interview for this position, due to a written warning you recently received on 2/2015. Therefore, you will not be eligible to pursue other opportunities until 8/2015. Thanks in advance and have a great day!

From: Pledger, Thomas J.
Sent: Wednesday, March 11, 2015 6:49 PM
To: ████████████
Subject: RE: Thank you for your interest in American Red Cross position of Lead Tech, Manufacturing, requisition # BIO52322

Good Morning ████████

I am replying to this e-mail to inform you that I will be on vacation from 03132015 through 03222015. I will be out of the state during this time. I will be returning to work on 03232015. If I need to take care of anything during this time regarding the position. Please contact me by phone at ████████████.

Thank You,

Author:
Thomas Pledger

From: ████████████████████████
Sent: Monday, March 09, 2015 5:24 PM
To: Pledger, Thomas J.
Subject: Thank you for your interest in American Red Cross position of Lead Tech, Manufacturing, requisition # BIO52322

Dear Thomas Pledger,

You are being considered for the position of Lead Tech, Manufacturing. We will continue to update you regarding the status of your application.

Requisition #: BIO52322
Job Title: Lead Tech, Manufacturing

EID:37

Now, notice where it says List Previous Warning, it lists an occurrence on 08/18/2014. Now all of a sudden, they pull that out of my file and write me up on 02/17/2015. This is exactly one day before the six month period would be up and this would have been a verbal warning for this write up. Yet, they waited until the day before to write me up in order to stop me from being able to interview for the Lead Tech position.

Tracey Denson killed two birds with one stone. She stopped me from interviewing for the Lead Tech job and she was able to use this as a further disciplinary action against me.

I was completely denied the position based on the write up. This was the third time in a year and a half that this happened. I was given a written warning after applying for a position. It became a running occurrence and very noticeable.

In March of 2015, after this occurrence, I became disgusted and decided it was time to do something about it. It was time that I took action. I came up with an extreme plan that would either prove what I was saying for months or it would get me fired. Either way, I had to try something.

Chapter 6

The Pen is by Far Mightier than the Sword

Taking action meant that I would need proof of the discrimination. So I bought a pen, and it was a special pen.

Take a very close look at the end of this pen. It is just not any pen, it is a video recording pen. My goal was to catch the discrimination on video. Needless to say, this pen caught some pretty fantastic things on video. But more than that, it caught on video several people who recognized that I was being discriminated against, because I was white. It is shocking what a few dollars can buy now a days.

After the lead tech, that was constantly reporting me to my supervisor, left the shift, a new lead tech treated me more fairly. He always treated me the same as everyone else. I believe that he was the fairest superior I had in the four years, that I worked at the Douglasville, Georgia, American Red Cross.

Chapter 7

Discrimination by Tracey Denson on Overtime

I sent Tracey Denson several e-mails desiring to work overtime, throughout 2013. She ignored me. Yet, she allowed other people to get overtime at their request.

This is just one of the times I asked her about working overtime.

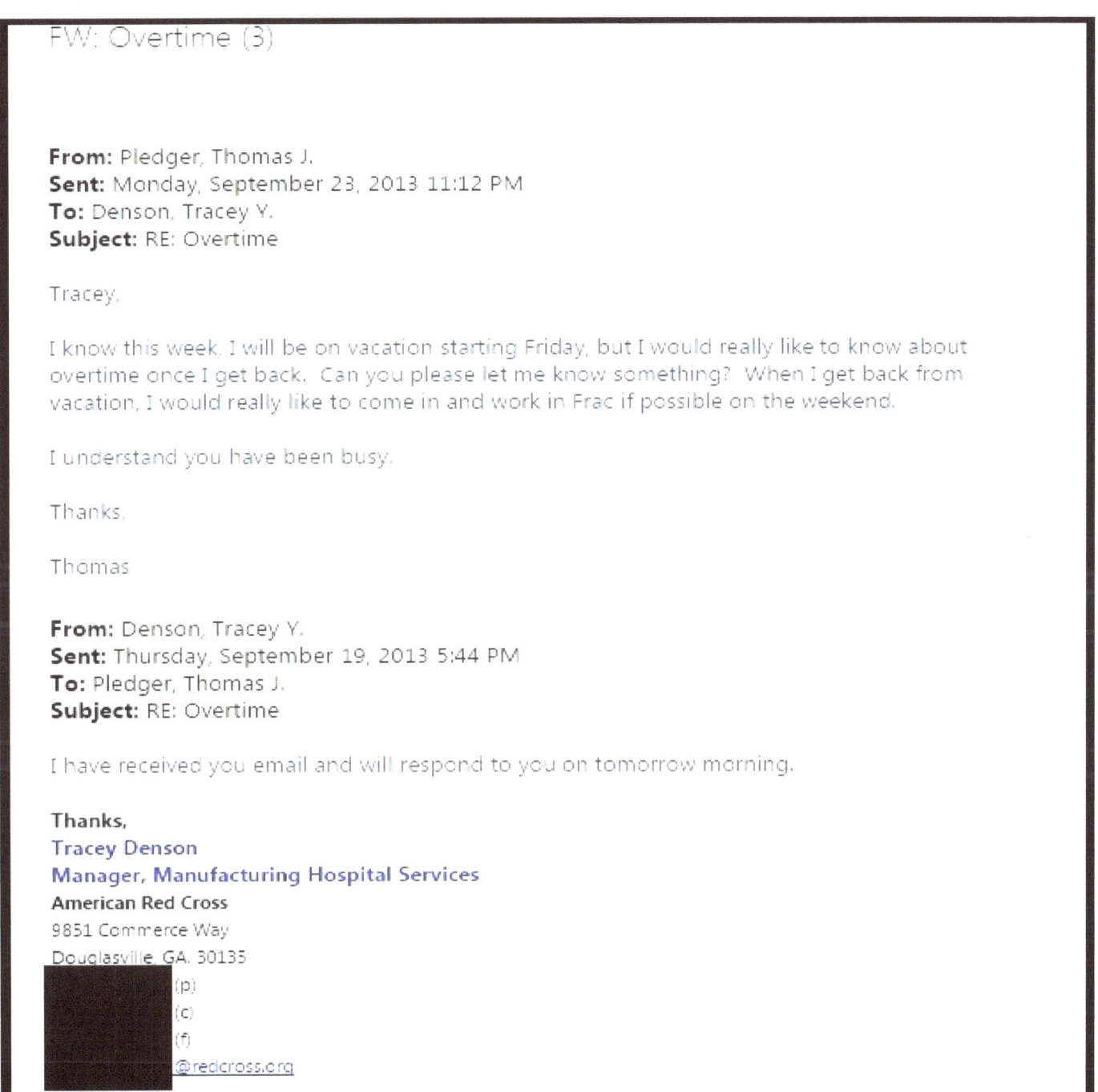

As you can see, this was four days after she e-mailed me, I did not hear back from her.

I e-mailed her again on September the 23, 2013 and she never e-mailed me back then either.

This was the final e-mail I sent before I gave up. I sent this to my supervisor.

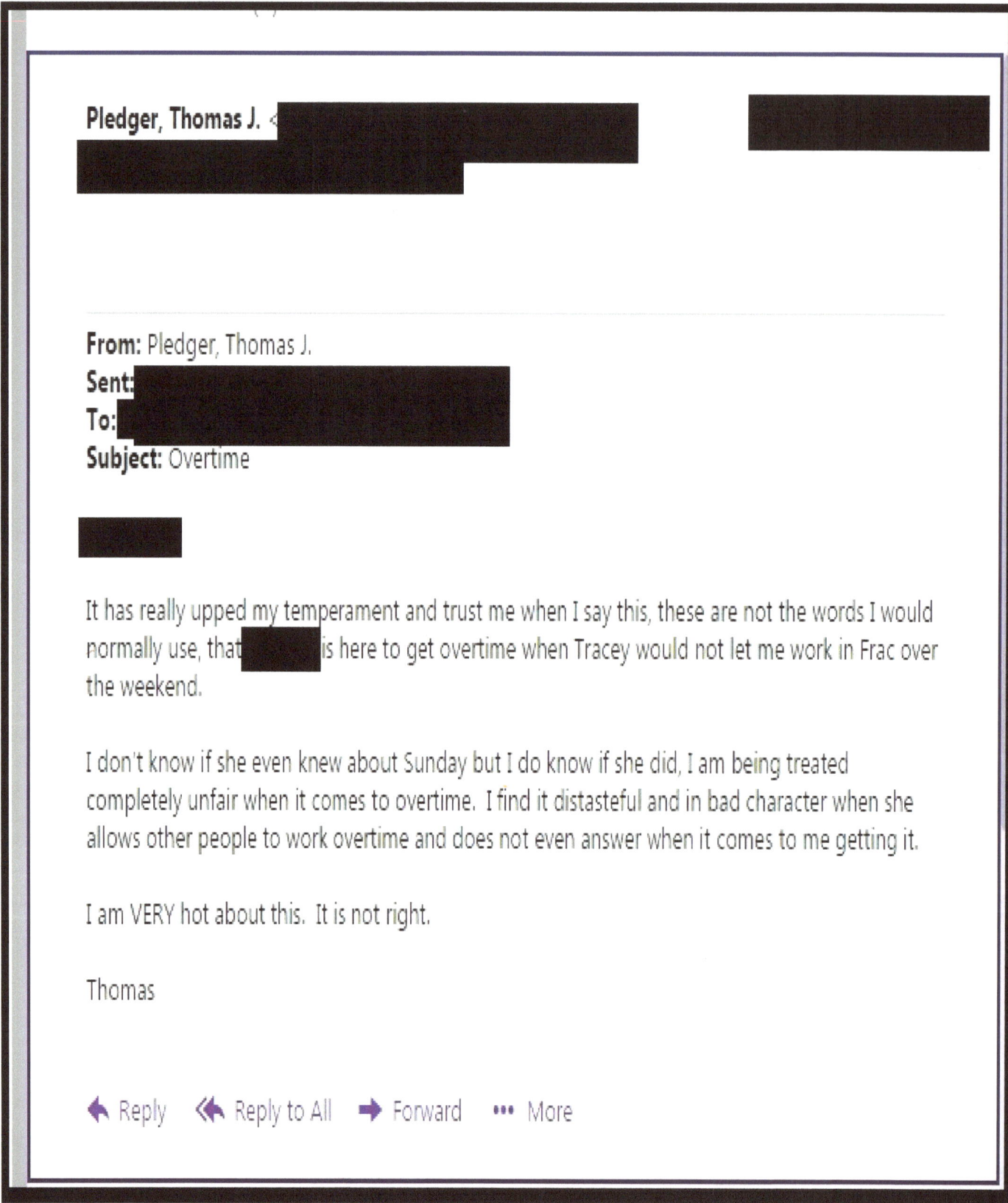

Pledger, Thomas J.

From: Pledger, Thomas J.
Sent:
To:
Subject: Overtime

It has really upped my temperament and trust me when I say this, these are not the words I would normally use, that ███████ is here to get overtime when Tracey would not let me work in Frac over the weekend.

I don't know if she even knew about Sunday but I do know if she did, I am being treated completely unfair when it comes to overtime. I find it distasteful and in bad character when she allows other people to work overtime and does not even answer when it comes to me getting it.

I am VERY hot about this. It is not right.

Thomas

↩ Reply   ↩ Reply to All   ➡ Forward   ••• More

I felt singled out, like my manager was discriminating against me when it came to overtime. Discrimination will leave a bad taste in anyone's mouth.

Chapter 8

Tracey Denson, 5 Days a Week.

I had heard from several people that we were soon going to five days a week. I contacted Tracey Denson with this e-mail. She deliberately ignored me and never replied.

Pledger, Thomas J.

From:	Pledger, Thomas J.
Sent:	Thursday, May 28, 2015 1:42 PM
To:	Denson, Tracey Y.
Subject:	Questions about 5 days a Week.

Tracey,

I have to ask this because it is really bothering me and making it hard for me to sleep. I have heard from multiple sources that soon we will all be forced to a 5 day a week schedule. I am asking you because I am tired of hearing from everyone other than management about changes that will affect my visitation with my daughter.

Less than a year ago, I went to a judge and asked him for my visitation to start on Friday when my daughter gets out of school and end on Monday when I take her back to school.

I am not married, I do not have a girlfriend and to be honest, I can not afford a baby sitter for her on the Friday or Sunday I will be forced to work. I received the approval for this change during the time I was trying to become a lead tech. It was the main reason I backed out of the fight over that situation for the lead tech position. With it being a 5 day a week position, I knew that I could not take the position. I understood, I was making the choice to go to 5 days if I took the position.

So as for a situation in this manner. Are you or anyone else trying to fight for us? Are you standing up and letting these people know that we have

1

This is page two of that e-mail.

lives based around our work schedules such as this and it is not right to force us to 5 days if we have based our lives around our schedules? As my dad used to say, if it's not broke, why try to fix it?

By trying to fix our schedules, has anyone realized that you are breaking the final good thing for some of us? Many of the employees are already upset with all the changes that keep being implemented but no one has the guts to tell you. I am telling you now, many of us are seriously upset with all the changes and rumors. We need your backing and guidance, please...

The crew in hospital services has always had the choice on their schedules. I am asking you to leave it that way for the ones on 3 and 4 days. I am going to ask you plainly, will you please fight for us and allow us to make the choice to go to 5 days as it has been for over a year now?

I have been a good employee for ARC for the past 2 years. I hardly ever get problems. I come to work unless I am seriously sick. I always pull my weight and I do my best to do as I am asked. I have asked for little or nothing in return. So I am coming to you today and finally asking for something because I need your help as does a great many of your crew members.

Will you please fight for us all to keep things as a choice for us?

We would all greatly appreciate your input and guidance.

Sincerely,

Thomas Pledger

As I said before, Tracey Denson did not reply to that e-mail, dated May 28,2015.

So, I sent another email, on July 22,2015. I added Arthur McDade III, into this mix, because I wanted a reply. With her boss watching, she actually replied. Her reply was simple, it is the union doing this, not me. Truth be told, everyone knew it was her. She was the one in charge of changing the schedules.

Pledger, Thomas J.

From:	Pledger, Thomas J.
Sent:	Wednesday, July 22, 2015 7:08 PM
To:	Denson, Tracey Y.; McDade III, Arthur
Subject:	RE: Questions about 5 days a Week.

Tracey,

I actually did not think this e-mail went through. I sent you another one. Although, I do think that your days third shift will be working is a little messed up. From what I read and understand. Third Shift will be overloaded on Fridays and short handed on Sundays. I suggest you review this before the final schedules are expedited...

I will however have to go to the union and discuss this with them. Although I already know there is little to nothing they can do. That is the reason you are rerouting me to them. You and Arthur are the only 2 that could help me in this situation and we both know it. That is why I came to both of you first.

Thanks,

Thomas

From: Denson, Tracey Y.
Sent: Wednesday, July 22, 2015 1:06 PM
To: Pledger, Thomas J.; McDade III, Arthur
Subject: RE: Questions about 5 days a Week.

Hi Thomas,

I do understand your position and how this change may impact you personally. I will have to recommend that you reach out to your Union representatives, discuss your concerns and give your suggestions.

Thanks,
Tracey Denson
Manager, Manufacturing Hospital Services
American Red Cross
9851 Commerce Way
Douglasville, GA. 30135
     (p)
     (c)
     (f)
     @redcross.org

From: Pledger, Thomas J.
Sent: Monday, July 20, 2015 10:36 AM
To: Denson, Tracey Y.; McDade III, Arthur
Subject: FW: Questions about 5 days a Week.

Tracey,

I sent you this e-mail a couple of months ago. You never replied, nor did I hear back from you. The schedule you are proposing is not helping me at all. I can not work 5 days a week on night shift.

1

This is the second page to that e-mail. The rest is on the previous page.

the only thing I can do is roll into a first shift position. With the new schedule, I have one of 2 choices, I can give you my notice or roll ███████ off of first shift speaking I have seniority. Even then, this will create an issue with ████████████

Although I love third shift and I asked you for help so I could stay on third shift. I have to do what is best for my child.

Thanks,

Thomas Pledger

From: Pledger, Thomas J.
Sent: Thursday, May 28, 2015 1:42 PM
To: Denson, Tracey Y.
Subject: Questions about 5 days a Week.

Tracey,

I have to ask this because it is really bothering me and making it hard for me to sleep. I have heard from multiple sources that soon we will all be forced to a 5 day a week schedule. I am asking you because I am tired of hearing from everyone other than management about changes that will affect my visitation with my daughter.

2

34

So, Tracey's reply is simple. I will blame it on the union. The union will blame it on us.
Then I don't have to deal with this situation. This marked the end of my patience and I would
report the discrimination. It was time I sat down with someone to tell them the truth about
what was going on, under the roof of the American Red Cross.

Chapter 9

Tisha Rumph, Arthur McDade III, Tracey Denson and Mary Deck

Unfair Schedule Sign-Ups and Discrimination Reported

By the time August had rolled around, the five day a week schedules were going into effect soon. So, they decided to do sign-ups for the schedules. Mind you, most people worked Monday thru Friday or Sunday thru Thursday. Yet, it was someone's bright idea to post sign ups Friday thru Monday, this limits employees opportunities to sign up for their preferred choice.

I will let my e-mail to Tisha Rumph explain it all.

This is the entire truth of how it all began.

Pledger, Thomas J.

From: Pledger, Thomas J.
Sent: Wednesday, August 05, 2015 5:33 AM
To: ███████ Rumph, Tisha; Denson, Tracey Y.; ████████████
Cc: ██████████ ████████; ██████████; Rumph, Tisha; McDade III, Arthur
Subject: RE: New Schedules

Ms. Rumph,

I am asking for an HR review of the below assigned issue. It is my belief that I was treated unfairly when it came to the schedule and our schedules are not finalized at this time. I had less than 24 hours to sign up for the hours or shift I wanted. Here is my explanation.

I came in on Monday July 27, 2015 and saw the sign up sheet mentioned in this e-mail. I work night shift. I did not get but one night to sign up. A deadline for what day the sign up sheet was to be taken and used to create the schedule was not posted. When I tried to talk to my first union rep. I was told that he had nothing to say to me.

I waited for the second union rep to come in at 4 am. Little did I know he was on PTO or something. So I could not talk to him about the issue or how much time I had.

When I came in at 6:30 pm on Tuesday July 28, 2015, and was going to sign up on the sheet for the hour I believed I could work, the sheet was gone. I was told that they had been working on the schedule all day and I had been placed on the schedule that I signed up for. The only issue is, I never got to sign up. I had less than 24 hours notice to sign up with no deadline.

I am asking that HR review this issue and assign me to Sunday thru Thursday schedule based on Seniority. I asked for 9 pm to 5:30 am as my second choice. I have did as D███ F███ asked and finally talked to ██████████ when he got back on Tuesday, August 4, 2015. ██████ talked with ██████ and ██████ and asked them to switch. They both said no.

I am asking that HR review this issue and come to the conclusion that I was in fact treated unfairly even though I followed every protocol to try and solve this issue up to now.

It is my full belief that EVERYONE else had at least 2 shifts or could talk to someone about the schedule within 2 shifts. This is not the case with myself and I am asking that this be reviewed because of how it was handled.

I am turning to HR as a last resort,

Thank you,

Thomas Pledger

Tisha Rumph informed me later that day that this was not an issue she could partake in. Everyone had the same amount of time. This was a lie and she was covering things up, the same as always. Human Resources always sided with American Red Cross. It was rare if EVER that they sided with the employees.

In response, I contacted Mary Deck by telephone, on August 5, 2015. I reported the discrimination. This is her e-mail reply.

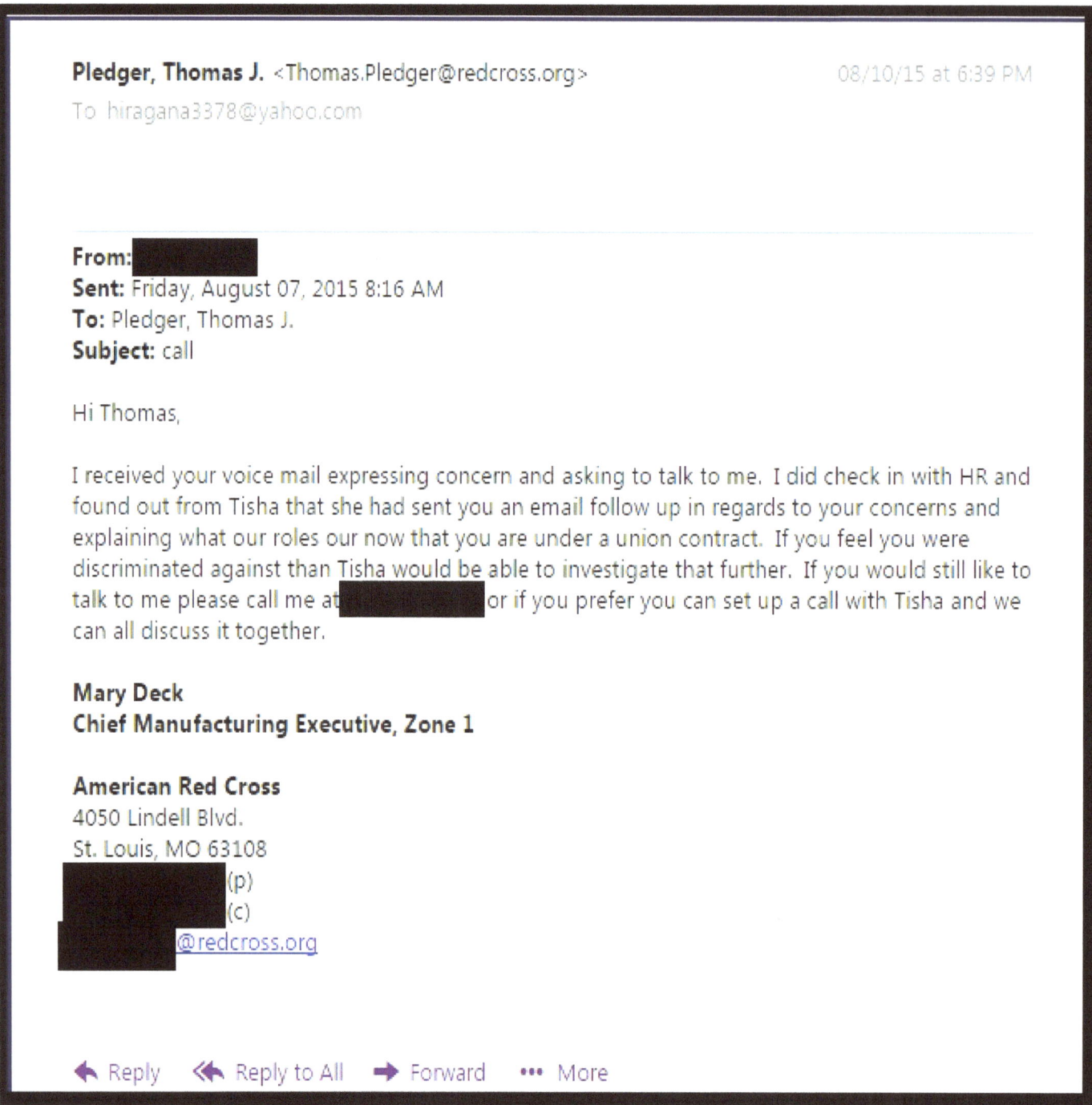

Pledger, Thomas J. <Thomas.Pledger@redcross.org>   08/10/15 at 6:39 PM
To hiragana3378@yahoo.com

From: ███████████
Sent: Friday, August 07, 2015 8:16 AM
To: Pledger, Thomas J.
Subject: call

Hi Thomas,

I received your voice mail expressing concern and asking to talk to me. I did check in with HR and found out from Tisha that she had sent you an email follow up in regards to your concerns and explaining what our roles our now that you are under a union contract. If you feel you were discriminated against than Tisha would be able to investigate that further. If you would still like to talk to me please call me at ███████████ or if you prefer you can set up a call with Tisha and we can all discuss it together.

Mary Deck
Chief Manufacturing Executive, Zone 1

American Red Cross
4050 Lindell Blvd.
St. Louis, MO 63108
███████████ (p)
███████████ (c)
████@redcross.org

↩ Reply   ↩ Reply to All   ➡ Forward   ••• More

In her e-mail, she says we can sit down and talk with Tisha Rumph. After I read this e-mail, I was informed by a union rep, I was under deep investigation. This means they are looking to fire me.

This is my reply to Mary Deck.

Pledger, Thomas J.

From: Pledger, Thomas J.
Sent: Monday, August 10, 2015 7:16 PM
To: Deck, Mary
Subject: RE: call
Attachments: ██████████

Mary,

I have been in constant contact with Management, Tracey Denson, Arthur McDade, Tisha Rumph, and the Union Executive ████. My concerns were surrounded by the 5 day a week schedule, seniority and how the sign ups were handled. Not to mention, the 5 day a week schedule has now cut my visitation with my daughter from 2.5 days and 3 nights to 1 night and a half day. I have found out that my concerns are not worth listening to. Therefore, I am warranted to give up on these concerns.

I will eventually wind up in ████████████████████████ because of my issues with the 5 days a week schedule. I have exhausted all of my means of trying to figure out what to do about my issues. ██████

██

In my honest opinion, the 5 day a week schedule, the signups and the way it was handled from the top down was VERY unprofessional. ████████████████████ Some people had 2 and 3 days to sign up, and by days, I mean shifts, while others only had a single shift. It was my opinion that this was discrimination. Many people say it is not but at the very minimum, it shows just how unfair the sign ups were handled.

██

I am one of the best distribution employees in the southern region. I do my job and I do it very well. When I needed just one person to have my back, no one did. ████████ tried but it was too late by the time he was able to.

I have decided to stay with my current schedule for 5 days a week and stop fighting the issue. ████

██

I think you should know how I felt about this situation and how it was handled. At this time, there is nothing for you to do or that I can do. ████████████████

Just to give you an idea of the type of person I am, I have decided to send you the original courts order. I want you to know that I am just not whining about the schedule, I am trying to protect my child. Not many men in my situation would.

Thank you for reading,

Thomas Pledger

I never heard back from Mary Deck. I knew then that my time was limited and I would soon be fired. However, I did not expect the management team to go so far as to frame me for a Ship Not Wand and use it to fire me, but they did.

On September 25, 2015, Tracey Denson finally offered me Sunday thru Thursday schedule on 3rd shift which is what I had been trying to get.

In the next chapter, you will find out she already knew she was going to fire me and I would never make it through my first week. I still have not figured out why she offered me the schedule I wanted, knowing she was going to terminate me before my first week of ever working it.

The new schedules started on October 5, 2015. I was terminated on October 7, 2015.

Chapter 10

Tracey Denson and the Framing for a Ship Not Wand

By September 2, 2015, I was informed that I had a Ship Not Wand by my supervisor. I told her, there was no way in hell. I do not make mistakes like that.

The claim is that I shipped an extra unit with order 2566631. I will explain the rest as I go. By 9/16/2015, I received an e-mail that stated I needed to join an online meeting to discuss my Ship Not Wand.

A ship not wand, in simple terms, is when an extra unit is put in the box without scanning it. I can tell you, I did not do this and that is the same thing I told the investigator. The video review findings verified my statement.

I received an e-mail to join a meeting about the ship not wand I was blamed for.

Pledger, Thomas J.

Subject:	FW: E-1779278 – Level 2 – SNW RCA meeting
Location:	████████, Conf ID 686665
Start:	Wed 9/16/2015 6:30 PM
End:	Wed 9/16/2015 7:30 PM
Show Time As:	Tentative
Recurrence:	(none)
Meeting Status:	Not yet responded
Organizer:	████████, BJ

Sent again

-----Original Appointment-----
From: ████████, BJ
Sent: Thursday, September 10, 2015 3:28 PM
To: ████████, BJ; ████████; McDade III, Arthur; Denson, Tracey Y.; ████████
████████ Pledger, Thomas J.; ████████
~~Sadler, Steve~~
Subject: E-1779278 – Level 2 – SNW RCA meeting
When: Wednesday, September 16, 2015 6:30 PM-7:30 PM (GMT-05:00) Eastern Time (US & Canada).
Where: ████████, Conf ID 686665

Join online meeting

https://meet.lync.com/americanredcross-redcross/bradley.vanwagoner/G9NCV9MY

First online meeting?

Problem Description:

Description

Problem Statement: A product was shipped, not wand to a consignee

On 9/1/2015, during a call from St. Joseph's Hospital, Order Management Tech BB discovered that there was an extra product in the shipping container that was not on the packing slip. After investigation, Donor Identification Number W200115815769003 was shipped by Hospital Services staff member TP on 8/31/2015 with order 2566631.

In addition, Order Management staff BB generated order 2567651 on 9/1/2015 and Hospital Services Lead Tech CW electronically shipped the unit to St. Joseph's Hospital on 9/1/2015 without initiating a Clarify Case or putting the product on electronic hold. The error occurred in the Southern Region Hospital Services

1

The meeting would be starting at 6:30 p.m. est. on 09/16/2015.

This is page two of that e-mail.

Department and Order Management Department on 8/31/2015 and 9/1/2015.

SQuIPP was unaffected since the product was suitable for release and the shipping container did not exceed the maximum volume.

CAP Due Date: 10/1/2015
Associated Staff: Thomas Pledger, ███████████████████████
Procedure(s) Violated: 21.3.122, System 11

Agenda:
-Problem Description
-Procedures
-Failure modes
-Elimination of Probable causes
-Root cause
-Hypothesis testing
-CA/EC Development

Associated Documentation:

E-1779278 Shipped   E-1779278   E-1779278 mpf.pdf
Not Wanded o...   upporting docs .pdf.

As you can read, it basically says I need to be there to explain what happened.

As I read further through the e-mail, I began to read the video review findings. Let's take a look at the statements.

The Video Review Findings.

Shipped Not Wanded/Wanded Not Shipped
Investigational Tool

Complete electronically...   **Problem Number: E-1779278**

Shipped Not Wanded   OR   **Wanded Not Shipped**   OR   **Reciprocal Error**
☒   ☐   *(shipped not wand and wand not shipped)*
☐

Customer Order ☒   OR   **Site-to-Site Transfer** ☐

Facility (City): **Douglasville**   **Date of Occurrence: 08312015**

Summary of Event: During a call from St. Joseph's Hospital, OM Tech, BB, was notified that there was an extra product in a shipment received by the customer that was not listed on the packing slip. The extra product (W200115815769003) was received with order# 2566631 that was shipped was shipped on 08312015. Additionally, the OM tech generated a new order that was used by HS lead tech to electronically ship the product. Product was not placed on hold and a clarify case was not initiated per the BSL. The error occurred in the Order Management Department on 08312015. SQuIPP was not impacted

Video Review Findings (if available): (3 products ordered/ 4 packed). The video show that the employee prepared the container, selected the coolant, and used the picking ticket to retrieve the products. During the shipping process the employee pulled each product from the cart, scanned it, and placed it directly into the counting tray. It appears that the employee only scanned 3 products, which is what the order requested.

If you skip down to the second paragraph, you can see that I shipped exactly what the order called for. The order called for three units and the video shows that I shipped three units. To me, that is all that is important. I DID NOT ship an extra unit.

If you are wondering about the blacked out area, I blacked out what ARC says "could have happened." The video shows I shipped three units. The order called for three units, so why are we discussing what "could have happened?"

I would love to tell you I beat this and I once again triumphed, but the truth is, I was framed and told to not be at the meeting by Tracey Denson. I was told sometime later that Arthur McDade III was the one who told her to do it, but truth is, I know Tracey did this and can prove it.

I called Tracey on my way to work, on September 16, 2015, to discuss with her about the meeting. She told me, "You do not have to be there, I have already taken care of it."

Taking my manager at her word, I did not go to the meeting. At about 7:00 p.m., I got a call on the floor by BJ. Remember the man who sent the e-mail on page 42? He was the one holding the proceedings for the meeting. His exact words were, "Did you not think the meeting was important enough to join in?" I told him that my superior had told me not to come.

I answered a few questions and after I hung up with him, I was pissed and went looking for Tracey Denson, in her office. I ran into Arthur McDade III and he told me that she had just went home.

So, I text Tracey Denson.

This is the text I sent and received from her.

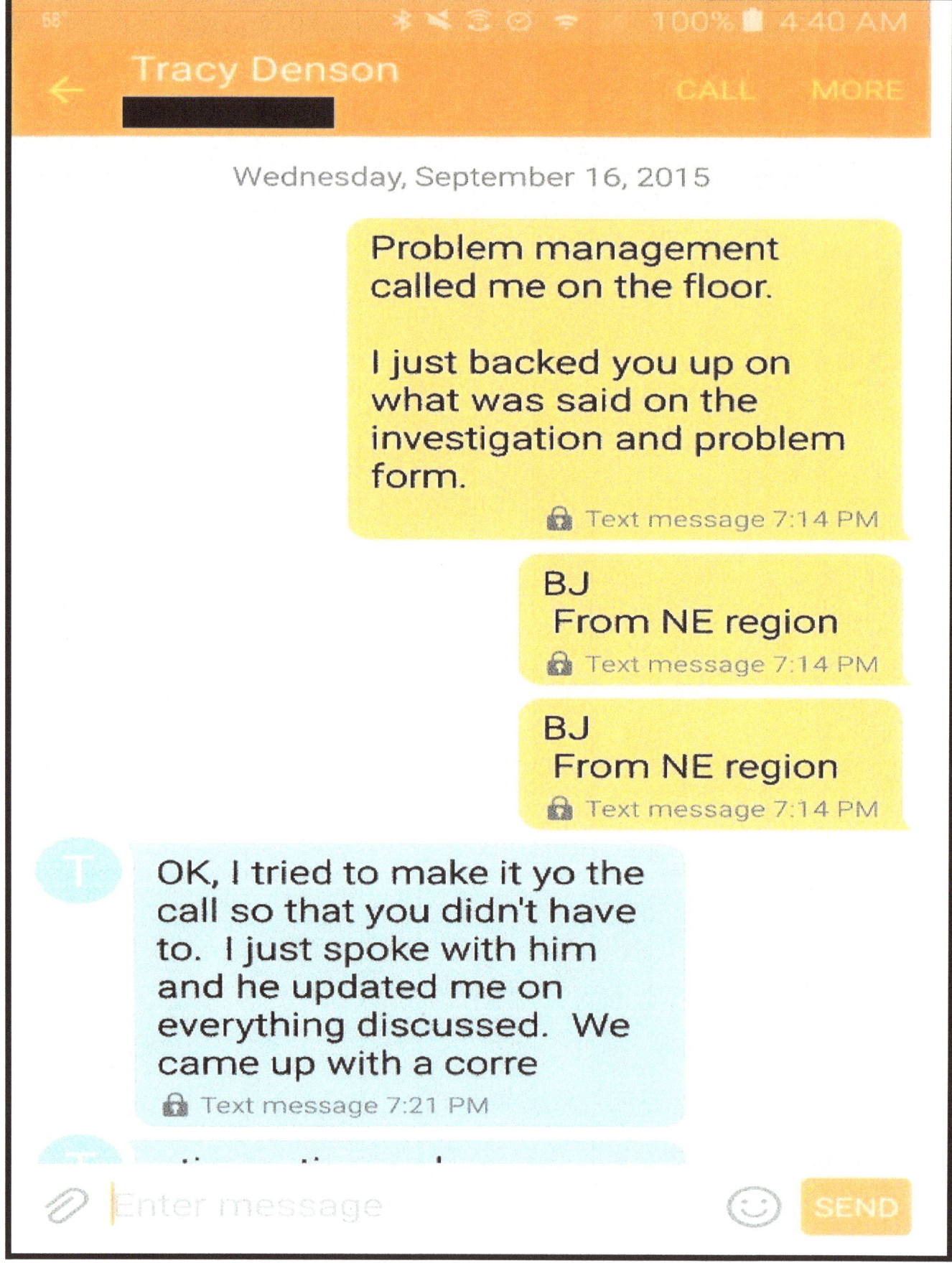

This is a second shot of that same text with the rest of her reply.

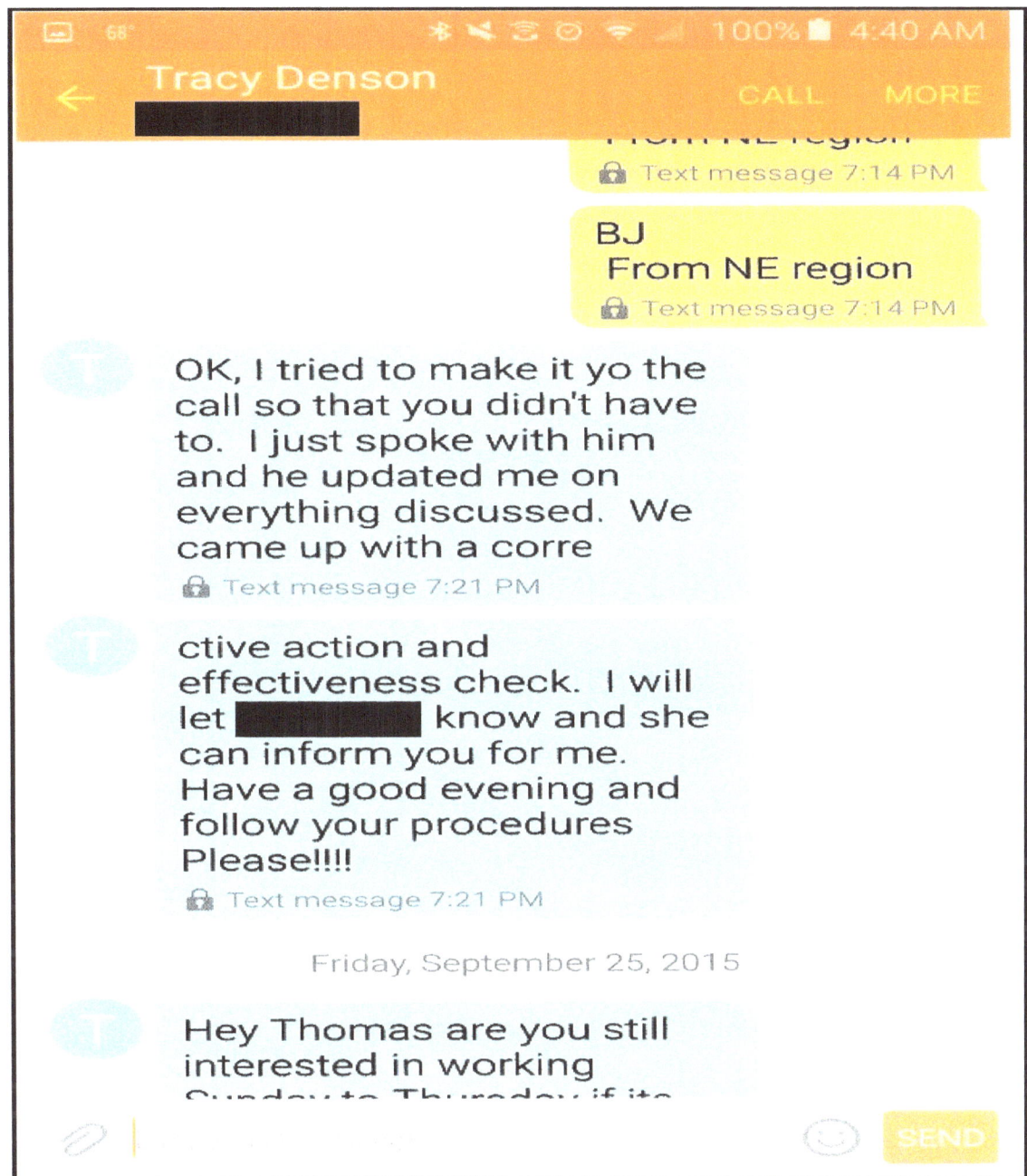

It says simply, "Ok, I tried to make it to the call so you didn't have to. I just spoke with him and he updated me on everything discussed. We came up with a corrective action and effectiveness check. I will let ******* (supervisor) know and she can inform you for me...."

This is the exact moment I realized that Tracey Denson had just gotten me fired or was going to fire me.

She framed me for a ship not wand, which I did not do. Then she stopped me from coming to the meeting about that ship not wand. She had effectively terminated me. It was just a matter of time.

Chapter 11

Discriminated, Retaliated Against and Terminated by Tracey Denson and Tisha Rumph!

On October 7, 2015 at 5:00 a.m. in the morning. Tracey Denson terminated my employment at the American Red Cross in Douglasville, Georgia. Her reason given was for my termination was the ship not wand.

The statement is here in my Termination letter.

Southern Blood Services Region
9851 Commerce Way
Douglasville, GA 30135

October 7, 2015

Thomas Pledger
67 Fulton Street SE
Atlanta, GA 30012

Dear Thomas:

You were hired on September 19, 2011, as a Manufacturing Tech II. Following compliance procedures is a critical component within Manufacturing Services and an expectation of each Manufacturing Tech II. On August 31, 2015, you failed to follow procedures by not performing a visual inspection or a final touch count when packing a product order for delivery. Consequently, your actions led to an extra product being shipped to the customer and created a ship not wand problem being logged by ARC.

On September 23, 2013, you signed a ship not wand memo which outlined the expectations of following said procedure. Specifically, you would "Perform a touch count each and EVERY time" as stated in the memo. You did not perform a touch count as confirmed on video footage. Notwithstanding the above, a review of your personnel file indicates that you received a Verbal Warning dated 1/21/15 for willful violation of compliance procedures; a Written Warning dated 2/17/15 for insubordination; and a Verbal Warning dated 8/19/14 for performance. Because of your actions on August 31, 2015 and your personnel work record, we are terminating your employment effective today.

A copy of instructions on how to access the HRIS system to view your pay information, EAP information, as well as information to The Work Number for employment verification is enclosed. Your separation notice is also enclosed. Your benefits are effective until October 31, 2015. You will be sent COBRA insurance information from The Benefits Service Center once your benefits end.

Sincerely,

Tisha Rumph

Tisha Rumph
Human Resources Advisor

cc: Tracey Denson, Manufacturing Manager
        Personnel File

Now, Tracey Denson and Tisha Rumph both lied on this letter about why I was fired. Let me tell you the truth.

The truth is, I was fired for reporting the discrimination to Mary Deck.

The date Mary Deck e-mailed me back about the discrimination was August 7, 2015. The date I got terminated is October 7, 2015. It is exactly 2 months to the day after I reported the discrimination. That is more than mere coincidence. That alone is retaliation.

Assuming that retaliation is not the case. Let's assume for a moment, Tracey Denson and Tisha Rumph terminated my employment, because of the ship not wand. If this is the case, then both of them DISCRIMINATED against me because I AM WHITE!

Every African American male and female that got their first ship not wand was given a FINAL WARNING for their first one. Yet, Tracey Denson and Tisha Rumph opted to terminate me for my first one. THAT ALONE IS DISCRIMINATION.

The following conversation is from a former employee that worked in hospital services for a while. The conversation was taken from a social media site. We had this conversation on February 3rd, 2016.

The conversation from that day will tell in details from another witness what they saw and heard. This is page one of three of that conversation.

Conversation started February 3

Thomas Pledger
What's up man

How u been

Thomas Pledger
I have been okay. What about you?

I'm great u know red Cross let me go also lol

Thomas Pledger
I heard from someone that you were not there recently.

You know I got a massive law suit against them right now.

Yea about to weeks ago

I heard I hope u win if u need me let me know cause they where unfair

Thomas Pledger
I need you...

You can prove the main issue of my law suit

Ok what I need to do

Thomas Pledger
Can you talk on the phone?

I'm at work right now

Thomas Pledger
If you remember. I got fired for my first ship not wand.

Yep then they lied about u didn't have to come to the meeting regarding

This is page two of three of that conversation on February 3, 2016.

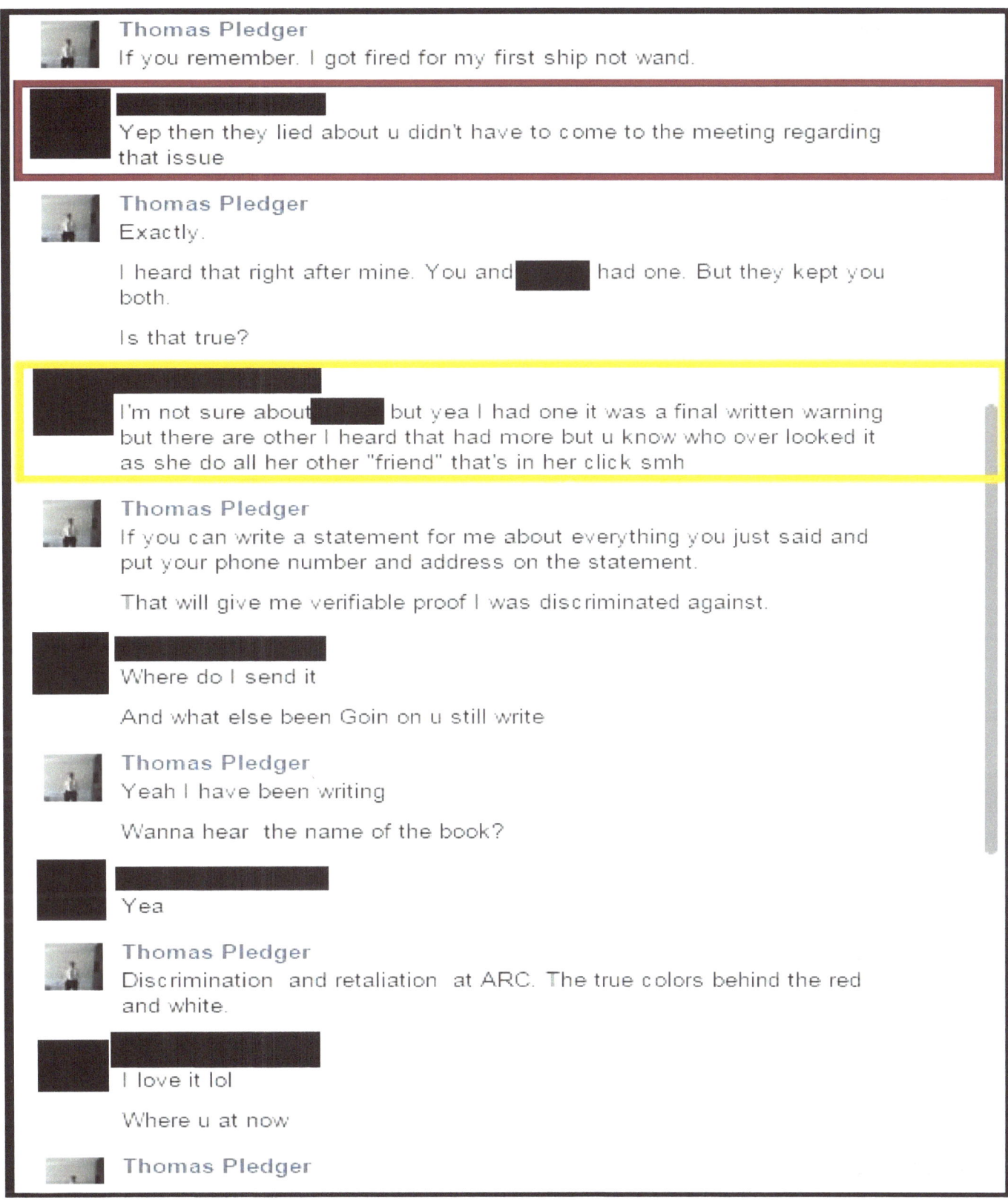

Thomas Pledger
If you remember. I got fired for my first ship not wand.

Yep then they lied about u didn't have to come to the meeting regarding that issue

Thomas Pledger
Exactly.

I heard that right after mine. You and ▮▮▮▮ had one. But they kept you both.

Is that true?

I'm not sure about ▮▮▮▮ but yea I had one it was a final written warning but there are other I heard that had more but u know who over looked it as she do all her other "friend" that's in her click smh

Thomas Pledger
If you can write a statement for me about everything you just said and put your phone number and address on the statement.

That will give me verifiable proof I was discriminated against.

Where do I send it

And what else been Goin on u still write

Thomas Pledger
Yeah I have been writing

Wanna hear the name of the book?

Yea

Thomas Pledger
Discrimination and retaliation at ARC. The true colors behind the red and white.

I love it lol

Where u at now

Thomas Pledger

In this page, you see that the witness says, there are other people with more Ship Not Wands than myself and yet, American Red Cross kept them. Again, I have proven discrimination against me. I put boxes around key points of this conversation.

In the red box, you can see where the person stated that "THEY" as in Tracey Denson lied about me not needing to be at the meeting discussed in Chapter 10.

In the gold box, you can see where the person stated, other employees had more than one and "SHE" referring to Tracey Denson covered those up so they could get away it. Her "Friend" as in employees she covered up things for.

This is page three of three of that conversation on February 3, 2016.

The letter, page one...

Subject: 6 Month Rolling Write Up Period and Ship not wand Policies at American Red Cross

To whom it may concern,

I worked for the American Red Cross for approximately 5-1/2 years. I was a Lead Tech at the time I left the company on weekend shift. I left the company on this date June 2015.

I knew Thomas Pledger. He was a great employee. He did his job as best to his knowledge as he could. Thomas was extremely knowledgeable and had a vast area of expertise in Hospital Services at American Red Cross.

6 Month rolling Period for Write Ups

The reason I am writing this letter is because, Thomas has made me aware that disciplinary actions/write ups were used against him during his termination that were more than 6 months old. Those write ups should not have been used. The entire time I worked there, any write up you received would essentially fall off after 6 months. If you committed the infraction again after 6 months, the tiers would start over. Granted, the write ups are kept in your file for filing purposes, but that is it. Those write ups are essentially dead after 6 months.

Example: If you were late for work 7 times, you would get a verbal warning. If you were late again an eighth time within 6 months, then you would get a written warning. If 6 months go by and you were not late again. The write ups would essentially be invalid. But 8 months after your second write up, you were late again, because it has been more than 6 months, the tier would start over at a VERBAL warning. You WOULD NOT get the next tier after the written warning.

My supervisor at the time, and for all the time I was there would preach upon these facts. All write ups and disciplinary actions would start over after 6 months. They could not and be used against you after 6 months. The facts are simple. Those write ups **SHOULD NOT** have been used.

Ship Not Wand Policy

The ship not wand policy at American Red Cross is simple. If you get one SHIP NOT WAND! You are given a FINAL WRITTEN WARNING. If you get a SECOND SHIP NOT WAND within 1 year, you are terminated immediately.

The Letter, Page two...

I witnessed on several occasions and heard about Ship Not Wands in Hospital Services. Every employee whom got their first Ship Not Wand was written up with a FINAL WRITTEN WARNING. *Every time, there was a Ship Not Wand, the employee violated a policy at American Red Cross.*

Examples:

The employee did not count the products before placing them into the box.

The employee did not use the red tray when an issue with a product was found.

The employee walked away from the desk during shipping and returned.

The employee did not start over when the employee needed another unit.

Yet the employee was only given a Final Written Warning for violating American Red Cross Policies. Only one employee was terminated for this issue to my knowledge and that employee had several Ship Not Wands.

I know this to be factual. Thomas Pledger never had a Ship Not Wand while I was at the American Red Cross. Therefore I find that his termination for a Ship Not Wand to be discriminatory. Every other employee whom got their first ship not wand was given a FINAL WRITTEN WARNING for their first SHIP NOT WAND. Essentially, I find it unethical to **not** follow the same procedures with one employee that you would follow with other employees.

I have known Thomas for several years and I know he always follows his beliefs and speaks truth. When he says he does not believe he did this, I believe him.

I will be out of the country on vacation until this date November 8, 2015. I am sending in my written statement and testimony because I believe that Thomas is right. If you have any questions, could you contact me after this date at the above phone number.

Thank you,

Signed █████████████████████████████

Dated 11/01/15

By reading this letter, you can see that it speaks to the gross discrimination, targeting, and retaliation, that I experienced while working at the American Red Cross.

This is an actual ARC document that proves the 6 month rolling period for write-ups. I highlighted the actual words in the document.

PER AGREEMENT WITH UNITED STEELWORKERS, BELOW IS THE ATTENDANCE POLICY FOR MANUFACTURING

TIME AND ATTENDANCE DISCIPLINE GUIDELINES:

It was mutually agreed upon that occurrences of tardiness will not be charged as a tardy if 5 minutes or less when returning from lunch or arriving to work.

TARDY

Unexcused Tardy/Early Departure (based on a rolling 6 month calendar)

- 3 occurrences – coaching
- 4 occurrences – verbal warning
- 5 occurrences – written warning
- 6 occurrences – final written
- 7 occurrences – suspension or termination

EARLY DEPARTURE

- 3 occurrences – coaching
- 4 occurrences – verbal warning
- 5 occurrences – written warning
- 6 occurrences – final written
- 7 occurrences – suspension or termination

Excused Tardy (based on a rolling 6 month calendar)

- 6 occurrences – coaching
- 7 occurrences – verbal warning
- 8 occurrences – written warning
- 9 occurrences – final written
- 10 occurrences – suspension or termination

ATTENDANCE

Excused absences (based on a rolling 6 month calendar)

- 3 occurrences – verbal warning
- 4 occurrences – written warning
- 5 occurrences – final written
- 6 occurrences – suspension or termination

Unexcused absences (based on a rolling 6 month calendar)

- 2 occurrences – verbal warning
- 3 occurrences – written warning
- 4 occurrences – final written
- 5 occurrences – suspension or termination

Updated January 15, 2016

As you can see, this proves write-ups were based on a 6 month period. Yet, I was fired using 2 write-ups that were over 6 months. ARC discrimination is at work here...

This is why I have decided to file suit against the American Red Cross.

I was a pretty good employee whom never had many problems. I have 5 of these. Some for a year, and some for 6 months.

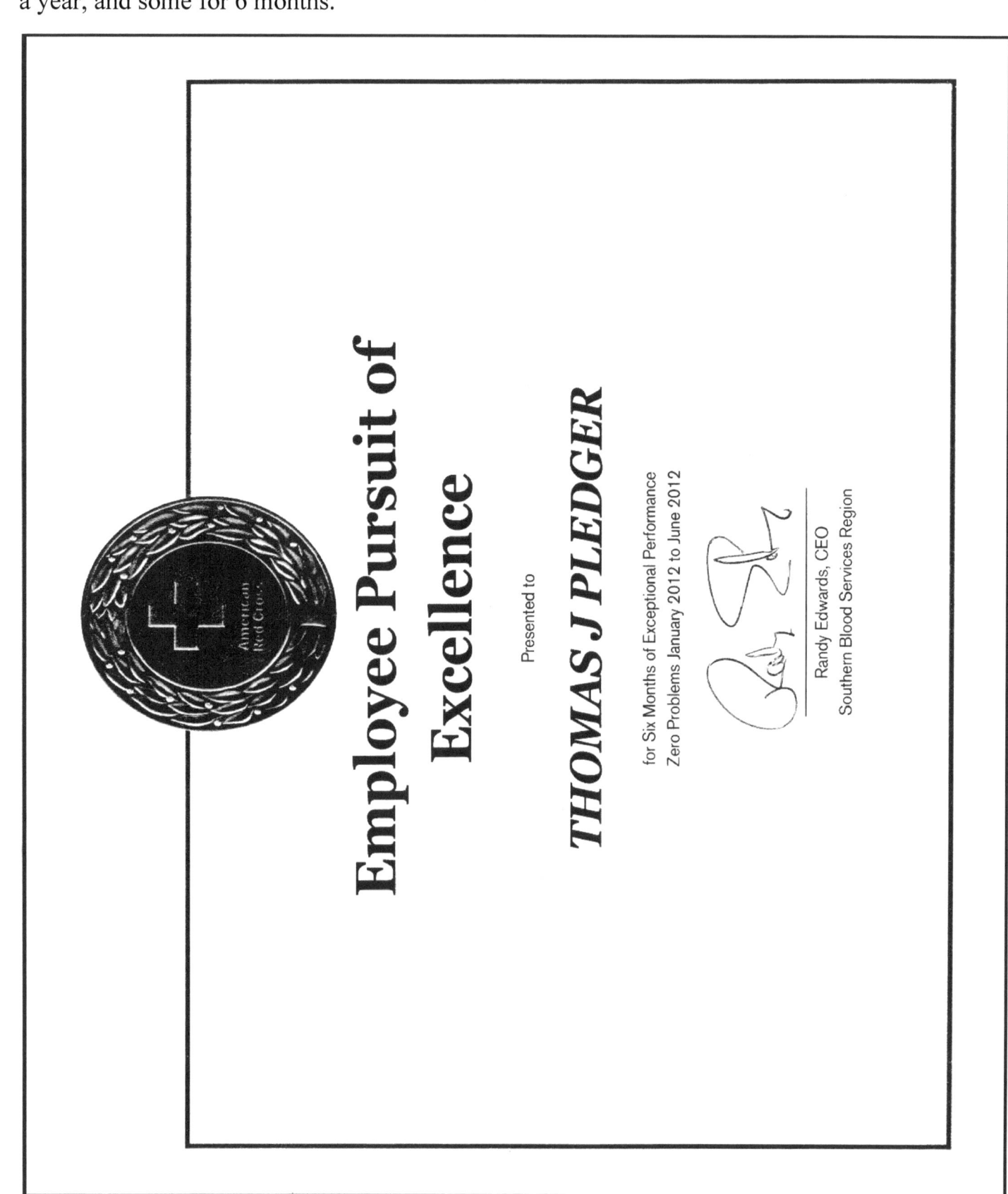

Employee Pursuit of Excellence

Presented to

THOMAS J PLEDGER

for Six Months of Exceptional Performance
Zero Problems January 2012 to June 2012

Randy Edwards, CEO
Southern Blood Services Region

Employee Pursuit of Excellence

Presented to

THOMAS J PLEDGER

Six Months of Exceptional Performance with Zero Problems
June 2013 - November 2013

Debbie Drozda

Debbie Drozda, Chief Manufacturing Executive – Zone 4
February 2014

Employee Pursuit of Excellence

Presented to

THOMAS J PLEDGER

January 2014 June 2014
Six Months of Exceptional Performance with Zero Problems
Southern

Debbie Drozda, Chief Manufacturing Executive – Zone 4
August 2014

Employee Pursuit of Excellence

Presented to

THOMAS J PLEDGER

Six Months of Exceptional Performance with Zero Problems
Southern Region
July 2014 - December 2014

Debbie Drozda, Chief Manufacturing Executive – Zone 4
April 2015

Employee Pursuit of Excellence

Presented to

THOMAS J PLEDGER

12 Consecutive Months of Exceptional Performance with Zero Problems

Southern Region

January 2014 – December 2014

Debbie Drozda, Chief Manufacturing Executive – Zone 4

April 2015

The EEOC investigation and filing from October 7, 2015.

EEOC Form 5 (11/09)

CHARGE OF DISCRIMINATION	Charge Presented To:	Agency(ies) Charge No(s):
This form is affected by the Privacy Act of 1974. See enclosed Privacy Act Statement and other information before completing this form.	☐ FEPA ☒ EEOC	410-2016-00137

_____ and EEOC

State or local Agency, if any

Name *(indicate Mr., Ms., Mrs.)*	Home Phone *(Incl. Area Code)*	Date of Birth
Thomas J. Pledger	▮▮▮▮	▮▮▮▮

Street Address	City, State and ZIP Code
▮▮▮▮ Rome, GA 30165	

Named is the Employer, Labor Organization, Employment Agency, Apprenticeship Committee, or State or Local Government Agency That I Believe Discriminated Against Me or Others. *(If more than two, list under PARTICULARS below.)*

Name	No. Employees, Members	Phone No. *(Include Area Code)*
AMERICAN RED CROSS	**500 or More**	**(770) 852-4972**

Street Address	City, State and ZIP Code
9851 Commerce Way, Douglasville, GA 30135	

Name	No. Employees, Members	Phone No. *(Include Area Code)*

Street Address	City, State and ZIP Code

DISCRIMINATION BASED ON *(Check appropriate box(es).)*

☒ RACE ☐ COLOR ☐ SEX ☐ RELIGION ☐ NATIONAL ORIGIN

☒ RETALIATION ☐ AGE ☐ DISABILITY ☐ GENETIC INFORMATION

☐ OTHER *(Specify)*

DATE(S) DISCRIMINATION TOOK PLACE
Earliest **12-01-2011** Latest **10-07-2015**

☐ CONTINUING ACTION

THE PARTICULARS ARE *(If additional paper is needed, attach extra sheet(s)):*

I began my employment with the above-named employer as a Distribution Tech II on September 17, 2011. Around December 1, 2011 to October 7, 2015, the above-named employer applied stricter standards regarding discipline. On August 8, 2014, January 21, 2015 and February 7, 2015, I received verbal and written reprimands. On August 5, 2015, I complained about racial discrimination to Human Resources. On October 7, 2015, I was discharged.

The reason given for my discharge was "failed to follow procedures by not performing a visual inspection or final touch count when packing a product order for delivery."

I believe that I have been discriminated against because of my race (White), and in retaliation for opposing an unlawful employment practice, in violation of Title VII of the Civil Rights Act of 1964, as amended.

I want this charge filed with both the EEOC and the State or local Agency, if any. I will advise the agencies if I change my address or phone number and I will cooperate fully with them in the processing of my charge in accordance with their procedures.	NOTARY – When necessary for State and Local Agency Requirements
I declare under penalty of perjury that the above is true and correct.	I swear or affirm that I have read the above charge and that it is true to the best of my knowledge, information and belief. SIGNATURE OF COMPLAINANT
Oct 07, 2015 *(Date)* *(Charging Party Signature)*	RECEIVED OCT 07 2015 SUBSCRIBED AND SWORN TO BEFORE ME THIS DATE *(month, day, year)* EEOC-ATDO

Discrimination can happen to anyone and all races. It is no longer a black or white issue. We as a society are always looking to the past for a definition of what discrimination is. In today's society, you cannot always judge a person by their looks. For actions have always spoken louder than words.

However, you can judge a company by how the people in charge treat their employees.

The next book in this series will be called:

Discrimination and Retaliation at a Job

The Steps An Employee Should Take to Protect Themselves and Prove It!

The Release Date is set for no later than June 15, 2016. I hope to have it out sooner!

This is my first book. It is a work of fiction. Check it out.

Shadows of Fear

Thomas Pledger

CHECK OUT THIS BOOK ON AMAZON.